The Beat
of the Drum

THE STORY OF DRUMS AND OTHER PERCUSSION INSTRUMENTS

The Beat of the Drum

By ROBERT W. SURPLUS

Illustrated by GEORGE OVERLIE

Musical Books for Young People

LERNER PUBLICATIONS COMPANY

MINNEAPOLIS, MINNESOTA

To Amy and Melanie

Copyright © 1963 by Lerner Publications Company

All rights reserved. International copyright secured. Manufactured in the United States of America. Published simultaneously in Canada by J. M. Dent & Sons Ltd., Don Mills, Ontario.

International Standard Book Number: 0-8225-0059-0
Library of Congress Catalog Card Number: 62-20800

Seventh Printing 1971

CONTENTS

The Big Parade

Have you ever seen a big parade? There are bands, drum corps, floats, pretty girls, and sometimes clowns. There is always great excitement as a parade goes by. Sometimes you wish you were marching along, too.

Part of the excitement at any parade is caused by listening to the drums. Most everyone is stirred by the deep, rumbling sound of the bass drum and the rapid, more exciting strokes of the snare drums. If you are like most young people, you get very interested when you hear the sound of drums going by in a parade.

The drums are part of the *percussion* section. The word percussion means the striking of one object against another. The drums, cymbals, triangle, and castanets are played this way. Percussion instruments are also played in more ways than just being struck. Some percussion instruments are shaken, while others are scraped. So when we talk about percussion instruments, we talk about instruments that are played by striking, shaking, or scraping.

When mother cooks a meal she usually starts out with meat, potatoes, and a vegetable. When she cooks them, she places salt and pepper or some other seasoning on them. What would have been an ordinary meal is changed with seasoning. Some people add mustard, horseradish, or a sauce. No matter what is added, the taste becomes more interesting to the eater.

Percussion instruments are to music as spice is to a good meal. They add that extra little dash that makes music more exciting. It may be the sound of a snappy snare drum roll, the crash of a cymbal, or the roll of the timpani that gives that little extra something that is so important. No matter which percussion instrument is used, the sound becomes more interesting and exciting to the listener.

Percussion instruments should be used the same as seasoning should be used—with good sense. A good cook would not pour a whole shaker of salt or pepper on food. A good composer would not add so much percussion that it spoiled the rest of the music.

How much do you know about drums and other percussion instruments? Are drums very old? When did they start? These are some questions this book will answer.

Early Percussion

Using all the information they can get, the experts have decided that one of the earliest instruments used by man was the rattle. Early rattles were probably made of nutshells, seeds, or small stones strung together in some way. Sometimes shells, seeds, or stones were put into a gourd of some kind. No matter how the rattles were made, they were all shaken by the player to make an interesting sound.

Many times rattles were placed on the ankles and wrists of dancers. As the dancers moved around, the motion of their bodies caused the rattles to sound. The use of rattles made dancing more interesting and exciting.

The *scraper* was another early percussion instrument. It was a very simple instrument. Scrapers were made of sticks, shells, bones, or gourds. Little notches were cut into the side of the instrument. The player then scraped against this notched part with a stick. Sometimes the instrument was held over a hole in the ground to add to the sound.

The *bull-roarer* was the name of another very early instrument. To early man it may have sounded like the voice of an ancestor, but to us it suggests the wind.

Like other early instruments, this one was quite simple. It was just a thin board with a long cord tied to one end. The player whirled the board around his head with the cord. While whirling, the board also spun around in a circle. The two movements made a roaring or wailing sound. If a small board was whirled around very quickly, a high tone was produced. If a large board was whirled quite slowly, a lower tone was produced.

The bull-roarer was used when ancient man wished to call upon the mysterious world of magic. It was also used for other reasons. In Malay, for example, it was used to frighten elephants and to keep them off the plantations. In some countries the bull-roarer has become a toy. Today, boys sometimes put a string through the hole of a ruler and whirl it around.

Rubbing instruments can make a number of squeaking or humming sounds. The Indians of Central and South America knew this when they made instruments of empty tortoise shells. They stopped up the hole where the tail had been. Then they made a most unusual sound by rubbing the shell with a sweaty hand.

In some of the Pacific Islands, the natives cut four teeth of different sizes into a rounded piece of wood. A player held the wood with his legs as he sat on the ground. He then covered his hands with palm juice from the many palms that grow in these islands. Then he rubbed his hands over the different teeth. Since the teeth were four different sizes, four different tones were heard.

Another early percussion instrument was the *stamping-pit*. It means just what it says—a pit to stamp over. A hole was dug into the ground and covered with bark. The musicians of that ancient day stamped on this bark with their feet to make a sound to go with dancing. Can you imagine the dull, hollow kind of drum sound that came from such an instrument?

Drums, Drums, Drums

The early drums were quite different from those of today. A drum is an instrument in which the sound comes from a skin stretched over a frame, or from a hollow body of some kind, like a tree trunk. If you had a barrel with no top or bottom, you would have a frame something like that of most drums.

The idea of pounding or stamping on a hollow tree trunk probably started around the time of the stamping-pit. Pounding on a tree trunk gave a much better sound than the stamping-pit did.

One type of early drum was the *slit-drum.* It was made by carving out or burning out the inside of a log of wood. When this was done, an opening, or slit, was left between the sides of the log. Quite often, more wood was left on one side of the log than the other. Because one side was thicker than the other, two different sounds were heard when the drum was struck on both sides. The higher of the two sounds would be heard from the thinner side, while the lower sound would come from the thicker side.

The slit-drum was played on the ground, with the slit facing up. Besides using these drums for music and dancing, primitive people also sent messages with them.

Some very large drums were made from sections of tree trunks. Some of them were as long as 10 feet. One of these tree drums may be seen in the Metropolitan Museum in New York City. It is a huge thing, about 7 feet tall and weighing about 700 pounds. In the islands of the Pacific known as the New Hebrides, every village has a *drum grove*. In some villages, many of these giant drums look almost like trees in a forest.

As time went on, some early man got the idea of stretching the skin of some animals over the hollow trunk of a tree. Striking the stretched skin with the hands gave a new sound. At first, men struck their drums with their hands, but later, sticks were used.

Today, when we think of drums, our minds turn to a parade. We also think about the military uses of drums. The Persians were the first to use drums for marching and other military reasons. They used a drum shaped like a hollow bowl, over which they stretched a goatskin. The first bowls were made of clay, although later the Turks made them of copper.

These drums were used in pairs. Since one drum was usually a little larger than the other, two different sounds came from the two drums. The sound from the larger drum was lower than the sound from the smaller drum. In time, these drums became the kettle-drums we know today.

The Arabs also used percussion instruments for military reasons, especially when they were about to attack an enemy. Their drums were usually made of pottery.

The people of Africa had drums of all sizes and shapes. Some had a round bottom and one skin over the opening at the top. Some drums were like barrels. They had two skins—one at the top and one at the bottom. The tree drums of Africa were very large, and much the same as those of the New Hebrides Islands already shown. A very interesting African drum was shaped like an hourglass. Drums of this shape were found in other countries, Germany for example.

The drums of Africa were used for many purposes. All Africans were fond of rhythm, and they used their drums to make music. They found great joy in beating out a rhythmic pattern and keeping time to it. Better yet, they enjoyed dancing to the beat of their drums.

Drums were used in some parts of Africa to tell a whole village what to do. There was a drum signal to wake up, a *food-beat* to eat to, and even a beat for drinking. The chief saw to it that a *work-beat* was sounded so that everyone went to work. The drums really controlled the lives of some Africans.

Village Drum

Telegraph-Drum

One kind of drum was used to send messages from village to village. The *telegraph-drum* was probably used more in Africa than any other part of the world. By using a code of drum beats, messages were sent many miles. The story is told that one of the inventors of wireless telegraphy got his first idea of sending messages without wires when he heard of the African telegraph drums.

11

There were other African drums called *talking-drums*. These were two drums of different sizes, one with a high tone and the other with a low tone. A small piece of iron was fastened to one of the drums to produce the sound the natives wanted. To some of the people on the west coast of Africa, the drums sounded like their language. They really thought the drums spoke real words.

The people of India always considered drums very important. There is a story that when Brahma, the founder of the Hindu religion, lived on earth, he gave a drum to an old hermit. The old man had been bothered by elephants and did not know how to get rid of them. Brahma told the old hermit: "If you beat on this side, your enemies will run away, while if you beat on the other side, they will become your friends."

The drum that was said to have been invented by Brahma had two heads with leather braces. The heads were tightened by slipping little blocks of wood under the leather braces. If the natives of India wanted to loosen the heads, they pulled the blocks of wood out from under the braces.

The drummers of India used to have a very strange custom. They put an *eye* on their drums. They used a dough or paste on the skins of their drums to make them sound louder as well as to lower the tone. This strange mixture was made of metal dust, boiled rice, and juice or water. Its color was black. The mixture was put in a small circle off to one side of the drum. The drum was struck on the clean part. How would you feel playing a drum with an eye?

Eye Drum

Bronze Drum

The *bronze drums* of Burma have been used for centuries. Both the shells and the heads of the drums were made of bronze. They were called "frog drums" by the natives, since most of them were decorated with frogs. These drums were played when rain was needed. This was because many native people thought that the croaking of frogs brought rain.

The *drum-organ* of Thailand is a very strange and interesting instrument. It was made of many drums tuned to different tones. These drums were fastened to a large round wooden frame. This frame was large enough for a man to sit in the middle of it. The drummer sat in the middle and played tunes by striking the different drums.

Drum Organ

Chinese
Bass Drum

The *bass drum* of the Chinese was an interesting drum. It was usually placed on a stand and it looked like a big orange. It was very important in parades, and its tone could be heard for long distances. The same thing is true of our modern bass drums. The first thing you can hear of a parade is the boom of the bass drum.

In Ceylon, a favorite drum was the *rabana*. It was a round drum about two feet across and about eight inches from top to bottom. This drum is played by the young girls of the rural villages even today. On holidays such as New Years, the girls dress in cloth with a beautiful floral design and a jacket trimmed with lace. To tune the drum to the sound they want, they heat it over a fire of coconut shells. The heat causes the skin of the drum to become very tight, and a high-pitched, exciting sound is heard. You can imagine the excitement this causes as the beat echoes throughout the village!

American Indians had many kinds of drums. The simplest was just a piece of rawhide which was beaten to produce a sound. Another simple drum was made of woven grass. Many Indian tribes made baskets of grass woven very tightly together. They turned the baskets over and beat on them. A deep basket made a rather good sound.

14

The Indians made drums by putting skins over any number of things. An old iron kettle, a turtle shell, a hollow log—any of these were used as drum shells. When people from Europe first came to America, they found the Indians playing drums made of earthenware, the same as people once did in parts of Europe and Asia.

The Indians were famous for their water drums. These were drums into which water was poured. The idea was that the water would make the drums louder and would improve the tone. The skins were put on the drums in such a way that they could be easily taken off when more water was needed. It was said that the tone of such drums carried at least ten miles over the surface of a river or lake.

No matter where drums were used, they were of great importance. When a primitive man was sad, he went to his drum for comfort. When he was happy, he showed his joy by playing his drum. He called upon his drum to protect him when he was worried.

From the earliest days, drums and percussion instruments had a magic meaning. They were used when man could not understand some things—like death. Early man covered up his feelings at such a time by playing drums. Even today, military funerals still include muffled drums, a bass drum, and a bugler to play *Taps*.

15

16

Drums of Today

The Timpani

The *timpani,* or as they are often called, the *kettledrums,* are the most important drums in the symphony orchestra. They are equally important in the concert band, but are not used in the marching band. During the 18th century some English marching regiments used small kettledrums, but the idea was never popular in America.

Timpani are often called kettledrums, because they look like huge kettles covered with calfskin. The calfskin is called the *head.* Today, some timpani heads are made of plastic instead of calfskin.

Timpani come in different sizes. The smaller ones are used to play the higher notes, while the larger ones play the lower notes. Timpani are different from other drums. They can change their pitch and can be tuned to different notes of the scale.

Notice the screws around the top of the timpani. These are used to raise or lower the pitch. To raise the pitch, the player tightens the screws, and to lower the pitch, he loosens the screws. On hand-tuned drums, the player must be very careful to turn each screw exactly the same so that equal tightness is found on all parts of the head. If he does not do this, he might strike a part of the drum that would give a pitch different from the rest of the drum.

17

There are several kinds of machine-tuned timpani. In Europe, a handle is sometimes used to tune the whole drum. In Italy, some drums turn on their stands to change the pitch. In America, pedal timpani are the best liked, although the pedal idea was invented by Ernest Pfundt, a German. He used a foot pedal which could be raised or lowered to make quick changes of pitch. It is possible to play a *slur,* or *glissando,* on pedal timpani. In a slur, the player slides from one note to another. Of course, you could not do this on hand-tuned timpani.

Two drums, one with a head 25 inches across the middle, and another with a head 28 inches across its middle, can play an *octave,* or eight notes. However, some modern timpani parts call for notes from low C below the staff to B♭ above the staff.

Notice that timpani play in the *bass* or *F-clef.* Many parts call for just the *tonic* and *dominant* notes of a scale. This means that in the key of F these two notes would be the tonic, or first note of the scale, and the dominant, or fifth note. The part could also call for the eighth note which is an F also, but is one octave higher than the first note.

Sometimes three or four timpani will be used. This happens when the music calls for very rapid changes in pitch. Sometimes the music is so fast the player cannot make the lightning-like changes needed to play the notes. Instead of trying to play these very fast parts on two timpani, three or even four are used. More than two timpani are also used when the music calls for more than two different pitches per measure.

Timpani are played with two sticks of about 12 inches in length. The handles of these sticks are slightly larger than the rest of the stick so that they can be easily held. The end of the stick used to

18

beat the timpani head is made of hard *felt* covered with soft felt. Felt is made of wool, fur and hair. It is interesting to know that the same felt used to cover piano hammers is used on timpani sticks. Sometimes,the beater is made of wood or cork covered with wool. Lambs wool and leather are sometimes used, and some music even calls for sticks with wooden heads.

The timpani, like most drums, are used to add something special to the music. All kinds of special effects can be produced. A sound like thunder is made by rapidly hitting the head with the beaters. Musicians call this a *roll.* A roll can be loud and frightening, or soft and mysterious. Whether the roll is loud or soft, the player hits the head very evenly with both sticks. When the sticks bounce off the head, they come to the same height. They fly farther away from the head during a loud roll than during a softer one, since the player uses more strength to play loudly.

The timpani are also used in *forte* passages (loud parts) to add to the sound of the wind instruments, especially the brass instruments. Timpani players also play solos. Listen to Aaron Copland's *Billy the Kid Suite* to hear an exciting gun battle played by timpani and snare drum.

Sometimes, the timpani are *muted,* or made softer by placing a cloth the size of a duster on each drum head. In this way, the tone is made softer, but not entirely stopped. This is used for special effects in music that calls for a soft, mysterious sound.

If a kettledrum is in fine condition and perfectly in tune, a curious thing will happen if the player hums the note it is tuned to over the spot where he beats the drum. In such a case, the drum will start to vibrate. Musicians say it is vibrating *in sympathy.* They use this term when drums vibrate to other musical sounds. If

the drum is tuned to F and the player hums this note, the

drum will vibrate an F, as well as another tone five notes higher. Because drums do vibrate to other sounds, players often cover drum heads when the drums are not in use to make sure that the sound of the vibrating drum is not heard while the other instruments are playing.

Some time you may want to hear what is meant by vibrating in sympathy. Go into a room where you see some drums. Then pick up a trumpet and play, or even play the piano. If you can't play an instrument, sing or shout at the drums. Even though you have not touched the drums, you will hear a sound from them.

Kettledrums have been in use since ancient times. They came from ancient clay pot drums, and as far as we know, were first used in the Middle East. During the Crusades, Saracen horsemen carried them on both sides of their horses. They used them to frighten the Crusaders as they went into battle. The sound of the drums made it seem as if there were more horsemen than there actually were.

Kettledrums were brought into Europe by the knights who returned from the Crusades. They were used to provide march music, together with pipes and trumpets. The drums were the small kind still used in the Middle East, with heads tightened by leather thongs. Larger timpani began to be used during the 15th century. The larger drums were first seen in Europe in the caravan of a Hungarian envoy to France in 1457.

About the middle of the 17th century, the timpani followed the trumpet into the orchestra. The English composer, Purcell, is given credit for first writing music for the timpani. At first, the timpani played just the tonic and dominant notes of the scale. Much of the music that is played today follows the same pattern.

A timpani player must be a good musician. He must have a fine sense of pitch as well as a fine sense of rhythm. He must watch the conductor carefully at all times. Above all, he must be dependable. He must make sure to play at the right times. Can you imagine what it would be like to have a timpani solo at the wrong spot in the music?

The Bass Drum

The big *bass drum* attracts a lot of attention as a parade goes down the street. It makes a booming sound and gives the beat for the marchers' steps. Since the bass drum controls the speed of the music, the bass drummer is a very important person. Some band directors feel a good bass drummer is the most important member of the band.

If you have ever heard bands on parade, you have probably heard the bass drum play this pattern. This is a drum beat that is heard all over the world.

Let's take a look at the bass drum. Actually, it is a large shell of wood with two drum heads. In parade, the bass drum is strapped to the body of the person playing it, while in a concert, it is placed in a folding stand which holds it upright. A bass drum measures two to three feet across the middle of the drum. The drums carried in parades are smaller than the drums used at concerts. However, some bands do use giant bass drums which are rolled about on a stand with wheels.

A narrow bass drum called a *Scotch* bass drum is used in many marching organizations. The narrowness and lightness allow the player to perform all kinds of fancy beats, as well as twirling of sticks.

The bass drum has no definite pitch, as does the timpani. However, the heads must be tightened to a point where the drum sounds good. Long metal rods with T-screws at each end are used to tighten the heads.

When used in a concert band or symphony orchestra, the bass drum is played with one stick. This stick has a big beater at one end and a smaller one at the other, so that a roll can be played. Timpani sticks can give a better roll than bass drum sticks, and they are usually called on for this effect.

The music for the bass drum is also written in the bass clef, but so is the music for the snare drum and the other percussion instruments, except for the keyboard percussion instuments. Here is a sample of some drum music. The bass drum part is written on low A or first space.

The bass drum also dates back to Middle and Far Eastern countries, where it had various shapes. Some of these early drums had large heads, some small heads. Some of them had a deep shell. Since they looked like barrels, they were called "barrel drums."

Bass drums were very rare in Europe until the 18th century when the percussion sections of Turkish bands became popular. In those days, the drum was sometimes played with a drum stick in the right hand and a switch of birch twigs in the left.

The bass drum player must have a good sense of rhythm and tempo. He is the one who must keep the tempo when the band is on parade. When playing in a concert band or symphony orchestra, he must follow the conductor carefully, since so many people depend upon his beat.

Orchestra Snare Drum

Marching Snare Drum

The Snare Drum

"Rat-a-tat-tat, rat-a-tat-tat" goes the *snare drum* as the drummer strikes his sticks against the head. This is the crisp type of sound that comes from the most exciting member of the drum family.

The snare drum gets its name from strings of gut, or narrow steel springs, called *snares,* that are stretched across the bottom head. The snare drum has two heads—the top, or *batter head,* and the bottom, or *snare head.* The batter head is usually thicker than the snare head, and is usually kept a little tighter. The heads are made of calfskin, although plastic heads are becoming more popular.

It is said that a Scottish drummer first got the idea of having snares. This drummer used a rawhide whip to strike one side of his drum, while he hit the other with sticks. Sometimes he would hold the whip against the one head while he used drumsticks against the other. Others must have liked the sound that was produced, because the idea spread. A little later, someone got the idea of placing cat gut strings against the head instead of a rawhide whip, and the snare drum was on its way.

23

When a drummer strikes the batter head with his sticks, the snares vibrate against the snare head. The snare drum gets its sound from the vibrations that are caused. When the snares vibrate, they form many smaller sound waves which rush against our eardrums and cause us to hear. The exciting sound of a snare drum as a parade goes by is caused by these waves of sound.

The snares can be adjusted from the side of a drum. A little handle is used to lower the snares from the snare head. When this is done, a snare drum sounds like a tom-tom. Some people call this way of playing *muffled drum.*

The snare drum has a shell of wood, or sometimes of metal. Shells come in different sizes. The drums used in orchestras usually measure around 14 to 15 inches across the middle of the drum, and about 6 to 8 inches from top to bottom. The snare drums used for marching bands are much bigger from top to bottom. The bigger size is used to make the louder sound needed for marching outdoors. Quite a bit of volume is needed when drums give the beat for a parade.

The snare drum is played with two sticks of hickory wood. They have rounded tips at the ends that strike the head. There is no felt at the end of these sticks as there is on timpani or bass drum beaters. Snare drum sticks come in different weights and different sizes. Some players prefer a heavy stick, while others like a light stick. Usually, heavier sticks are used when playing in a marching group than when playing in a concert organization. When music is played indoors, it is heard much easier and a drummer does not need to play as loud as he does outdoors. Outside, both a bigger drum and bigger sticks are used so the sound will carry. Whatever size sticks the player uses, he makes sure that they are heavy enough for him to bring out the full tone of the drum he is using.

As far as we know, drumsticks were first used by the Egyptians. Their drumsticks were not like ours, however. They were curved, while ours are straight.

24

Before bugle calls were used in armies to tell the soldiers what to do, orders were given by the drums. There were special drum calls which the soldiers recognized, the same as men recognized bugle calls later.

Back in 1775, William Dramand, the drummer of the Lexington militia, beat the call "To Arms" which gathered the men for the battles of Lexington and Concord. A drum gave the order for "the shot heard round the world" which started the American Revolution.

A snare drummer must have strong, relaxed wrists. Much of the time the snare drummer must play a roll. This is done by making two strokes of even strength with one hand, and then two with the other. The way the drummer uses his sticks is shown. L means left stick, and R means right stick. A roll would be like this: L L R R L L R R L L R R.

A good player can start a roll very, very slowly. He can gradually get faster and faster until he is playing so fast you can hardly believe it. When a drummer is playing slowly, musicians say his roll is *open.* When he is playing very quickly, they say his roll is *closed.*

A good snare drummer learns many interesting ways of using his sticks. Drummers call these different stickings *rudiments.* There are 26 rudiments. This is the number of ways of playing that the *National Association of Rudimental Drummers* decided was necessary to play all kinds of music. This association was formed by a group of musicians to promote good drumming. In order to join, a drummer must learn 13 required rudiments, and must agree to encourage others to learn how to play properly.

The rudiments have some funny sounding names. There are *flams* ♪♩ and *drags* ♫♩ . One name that young drummers like is *parradiddle.* A parradiddle sounds just like the word when played by a good drummer.

The Tenor Drum

The *tenor drum* is a large drum like a big snare drum. It is something like the large 18th century drum. This drum had a deep wooden shell and had no snares.

The tenor drum of today has no snares either. While it is about as big from top to bottom as a large snare drum, the distance across the head is usually greater—maybe 17 to 18 inches.

The tenor drum has a strange dull sound, different from the sound of any other drum. Its tone is heavier and duller than the tone of the snare drum. It sounds something like the bass drum, but does not have as full a tone. It is played with felt, or soft-headed drum sticks.

The tenor drum started in the army and is still used for marching purposes. You can count on seeing and hearing tenor drums whenever a drum corps marches by.

The Tambourine

Did you know that the *tambourine* is a drum? It has only one head, of course. This head is stretched over a hoop of wood. Around the side of the hoop, a number of holes are cut into the wood. A number of metal jingles are placed in these holes. These jingles are like little cymbals that sound when the instrument is played. The sound of the jingles always helps us to know the tambourine is playing.

While tambourines are made in many sizes, the ones used in an orchestra usually measure 10 to 12 inches across the head. The head is made of tough skin of some kind, usually sheep or goat skin. The head is fastened to the hoop, which is about 3 inches from top to bottom, by nails with large heads.

The tambourine may be played in several ways. It may be struck with the knuckles of the hand. This makes both the head and jingles sound. It may be shaken, in which case just the jingles

27

sound. It can be laid on the knee of the player, and struck on the head by fingers of both hands, or struck by the fingers on the edge of the hoop. It is possible to strike it against the body, and then to hold it out from the body while shaking it. It is even possible to make a roll on the tambourine. To do this, the thumb or finger is moistened and rubbed around the edge of the head. During such a roll, only the jingles sound.

The tambourine came from Arabia. The Arab tambourine with one head often had a snare and jingles. It came to Europe during the Crusades, and at that time was called a *timbrel*. The name may have come from the Bible, for the timbrel of the Bible was a type of tambourine. After a period of popularity, there came a time when tambourines were not used much in Europe. When Turkish military bands became popular during the 18th century, the tambourine once more came into use.

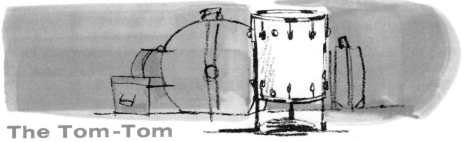

The Tom-Tom

The *tom-tom* began to be used in jazz music during the 1920's. It was like African native drums, and was copied from them. You can usually find one or two among the instruments of a dance band drummer.

Today, tom-toms come with two heads, but some drummers take the lower head off the drum. They say they like the sound with one head better. The distance across the drum and from top to bottom is usually about the same—from 12 to 16 inches. The tom-tom has no snares. It is played with snare drum sticks although at times a drummer will use sticks with felt beaters.

Traps

Dance band drummers use a number of drums, cymbals, and tom-toms to play the drum part for dance music. The complete outfit is known as a set of *traps*. One drummer using traps can play as many as seven or eight percussion instruments all by himself.

To see how this is possible, look at the picture of a trap set. The drum to the far right is a tom-tom. Next to the tom-tom is the bass drum. Notice the pedal on the bass drum. The drummer plays the bass drum part with his foot. Fastened to the bass drum is another tom-tom. This is smaller than the one to the far right. Tom-toms are used in different sizes to vary the drum music. It is possible to get much more interesting sounding beats when the two tom-toms have different pitches. The smaller tom-tom, of course, gives a higher sound than the larger one.

The snare drum is the small drum to the left. You can see a pair of drum sticks on it, as well as a pair of wire *brushes*. Brushes are used when slow, soft music is played.

Included with a good trap set are several cymbals. Notice the ones at the far left. These are matched cymbals. Drummers call them *hi-hat cymbals*. They play them with the left foot. Remember, the right foot is busy with the bass drum. The cymbal between the snare drum and the small tom-tom is a *crash cymbal,* and the one fastened to the bass drum is called a *ride cymbal*. The crash cymbal and the ride cymbal are not the same size. Will the sounds coming from them be the same, or different?

Percussion
from South of the Border

South American music with its catchy beat and flashing melodies is quite interesting to the people of North America. There are several drums that are used for this kind of music. One type of drums used are called *timbales*. Their shells are made of steel, and they have only one head. The drummer usually plays a large one and small one at the same time to get different sounds.

The largest of the drums used with South American music is called the *conga* drum. Sometimes it is known as the *tambora*. It is much longer than it is wide. The drum is slightly smaller at the bottom, or open end. One end is open, since these drums only have one head. The player often holds the drum by a cord which fits around his neck. Sometimes he puts it on the floor and uses both his fingers and hands to play very catchy rhythms. These drums have wooden frames.

Bongo drums are smaller than conga drums. They are not very big from top to bottom. They come in different sizes. The player can use two or three to produce different pitches. The shells are made of wood, and the drums are joined together. These drums are held between the knees, and patterns are played by the fingers and palms.

Here are two beat patterns you may want to try on South American drums. The first one would sound well with a kind of music we call a conga. It goes like this

When you strike the drum, play the beats in the part of the drum marked here.

The first and third beats are played on one side of the drum, the second at another part, and the two notes that come on four near the center.

The second beat you might want to try goes with calypso music. It looks like this:

When you play it, play the left hand louder than the right and the rhythm will sound as it should.

In addition to using special drums, the music from "south of the border" calls for other special instruments. Here are some of the most common.

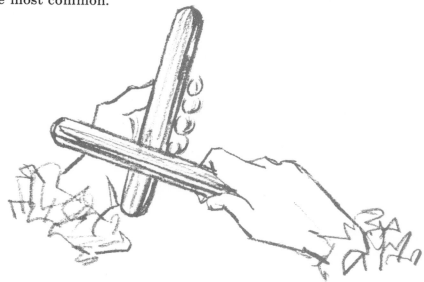

Claves (CLAH-vays) are small polished sticks of wood about 6 to 8 inches long. They are usually made of *rosewood,* a hard wood which gives off an interesting clicking sound. One of the sticks is rested between the thumb and fingers of the left hand, which is made into a loose fist and turned up. The second stick which is held in the right hand strikes the other stick with a fast light stroke.

The clave beat, which is usually found in music from South America, Mexico, and the islands of the Caribbean, looks like this.

Maracas are another percussion instrument favored by our neighbors to the South. The ancestors of our present-day maracas were the simple rattles of ancient times which were filled with seeds or small stones.

Maracas are made from a pair of gourds filled with shot. There are handles attached to the gourds so that the player can hold them. A gourd is held in each hand so that the player can shake one first, then the other. A short flick of the wrist and lower arm is used to make the playing motion. The part that the maracas play usually looks like this.

This part does not have the accents of the calypso beat shown earlier.

The *guiro* (GWEE-ró) is a hollow gourd about a foot in length. Small ridges are cut into one side of the gourd, and holes are cut into the other side. A thin stick is used to scrape back and forth across the ridges. The air inside the gourd adds to the scraping sound.

Also used is an instrument called the *shaker*. It is a large gourd, often hand carved and highly polished. Held in both hands, it is used to produce a tone something like the maracas.

34

Another instrument is the *cowbell*. Yes, the cowbell! Think of the cowbell on "old Bossie." Remove the clapper, and you've got just what is needed. The cowbell is played by striking it with the snare drum sticks.

Since the music of South America, Mexico, and the islands of the Caribbean area has been influenced by the music of Spain, one more instrument belongs in this section. This instrument has long been known in Spain. It is the *castanet*. Castanets come in pairs so they can be clicked together. The word castanet means chestnut, the wood from which castanets are usually made.

Castanets are small pieces of hollow wood shaped like a shallow cup. Holes are drilled through the wood and a brightly colored cord is pulled through the holes. The player uses the cord to hold the castanets in his fingers. Castanets are often used to accompany dancing. The dancer clicks the castanets together with her fingers as she moves about.

In the orchestra they are played a little differently. They are fastened onto a piece of wood with a handle. They are usually held in the right hand. The player shakes them with this hand, and sometimes strikes them against the palm of the left hand if he wants to bring out a certain note.

Keyboard Percussion

Did you know there are percussion instruments that look like a piano keyboard? In fact, there are people who say that a piano is a percussion instrument, since its keys are struck when the player's fingers come down. Only one of these keyboard percussion instruments is played with the fingers on keys as the piano. But they are all keyboard percussion. Let's find out why.

Here is a picture of part of a piano keyboard. Notice how the black keys fall into groups of twos and threes. Notice where the white keys are, and where the black keys are. The names of the notes are there for you to see. Keep this picture in mind as we talk about keyboard percussion, because the notes on these other instruments are arranged in exactly the same order as the notes on the piano.

The *xylophone* (ZI-lo-fone) is a keyboard percussion instrument. Here is a picture of the xylophone. Notice how the xylophone reminds you of the piano keyboard. Can you see why it is called a keyboard percussion instrument?

Xylophone comes from two Greek words, xylon meaning wood, and phone meaning sound. The word xylophone then, means sound of wood. This is a very old instrument and was known to primitive man.

A very simple form of xylophone was made when early man placed some slabs of wood on the ground and beat them with sticks. Sometimes, he dug a hole underneath the wood. This helped make the sound louder. As man grew wiser, he made a log xylophone in which the wooden bars were laid on two logs. If the slabs of wood were of the same width and thickness, the shorter bars sounded the higher notes, and the longer bars sounded the lower notes.

Every vibrating bar of wood has two *nodes*. These are places where the wood does not vibrate to produce a good tone. If the wood is struck at the node, the tone will sound dead. Because of this, on the xylophone of today, the wooden bars are fastened to the wooden frame at the nodes. A cord runs through the bars to hold them to the frame.

There is an interesting experiment that you could try if you had a xylophone. You could sprinkle some fine soap powder on the bars. The next step would be to strike the middle of the bars with a *mallet,* one of the sticks used to play the xylophone. The powder would fly off the bars, except at two small spots on each bar. Here, where the wood does not vibrate as much, the soap powder will remain. The two small spots where the soap powder remains would be the nodes.

When the xylophone is played with two hard sticks, it can be played very, very quickly. The tone is dry and, of course, it has a wooden sound. The notes also seem to have a sort of clicking sound.

Although tubes under the bars help make the tone louder, the xylophone cannot hold a tone for a very long time. If a player wants to play a long note, he has to hit the bar for the note with one mallet after the other, over and over until the note is finished. This is very much the same thing a timpani player does when he plays a roll.

In 1927, xylophones were greatly improved when it was discovered that scraping a small piece of wood from under the center of each bar made it possible to improve the tone of the instrument. This also made it possible to control the pitch of each little bar much easier than with the older instruments.

The xylophone is used for comic or unusual effects. You might want to listen to *Danse Macabre* by Saint-Saens to hear the xylophone imitate the sound of bones. This was the first serious piece of music in which the xylophone was used.

The *marimba* is very much like the xylophone except it has a much larger sound box for each note. Notice how the sound pipes for the marimba hang down much lower than those of the xylophone. These sound pipes, or boxes, are closed at the top, but at the bottom there is a small opening covered with skin. Striking a note causes the box to vibrate and the skin starts a buzzing sound.

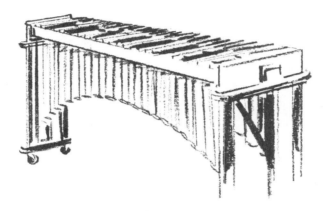

It is not easy to tell a marimba from a xylophone, since they are so much alike. How can you tell them apart? We have already said that the marimba hangs down much lower than the xylophone. It also sounds one octave lower in pitch. Even though the bars of the two instruments may be the same length and width, the notes will sound an octave apart. This is because the bars of the xylophone are thicker in the middle section than the bars of the marimba. Usually, wooden bars with closer and straighter grain lines are picked for the xylophone.

A xylophone can be used without resonators, or the sound boxes seen underneath the instrument; the marimba cannot. The xylophone sound is brilliant and does not last long. The marimba sound is more mellow and lasts longer. The xylophone is better suited to quick rapid music. The marimba is at its best when played with four, six, or eight mallets. A fast roll is especially pleasing to hear when played with a number of mallets.

The *glockenspiel* (GLOCK-en-schpeel) or *orchestra bells* looks like the piano keyboard. The bars of this instrument are made of metal instead of wood, and usually there are no resonators. The tone of these bells is quite sweet and pleasing to the ear. You might want to listen to the *Sorcerers Apprentice* by Dukas or the *Chinese Dance* from Tchaikovsky's *Nutcracker Suite* to hear the glockenspiel or orchestra bells.

Bell-lyra

Orchestra Bells

Today the word glockenspiel also means *bell-lyra*. Here is a picture of one of these glockenspiels. Notice how all the bars are fastened together. Notice also that there are no tubes under the bars to help the sound carry. In fact, no help is needed since it can be heard above all the instruments of the marching band. The tone is very brilliant and bell-like.

The glockenspiel is carried upright in the marching band. A belt fits around the body of the player, and the end of the instrument fits into a special part of the belt. Usually, white horse hair plumes are fastened to both sides of the instrument, although sometimes streamers with school colors are used instead.

The instrument is struck with hard rubber mallets. It usually plays melody, although sometimes it is called upon to play another part of the music.

Look at the back of the bars of a glockenspiel some time. Notice how the metal has been scraped to get the exact tone and pitch the instrument maker wanted.

The *vibraphone* is quite similar to the xylophone and marimba. However, there are a few differences. The bars are made of metal instead of wood. Underneath each bar is a little propellor, and underneath each propellor is a tube that helps make the tone stronger. The propellors are driven by an electric motor.

The tone of the vibraphone is very clear. It is possible to have a *vibrato* on the vibraphone the same as on the violin. On the violin the finger rocks back and forth to produce a vibrato. On the vibraphone, the electric motor is turned on to make a vibrato. Here is a note without a vibrato ——————— . Here is the same note with a vibrato 〜〜〜〜〜 . The vibrato makes the music sound much richer and more interesting. Just by changing the speed of the motor, the speed of the vibrato played by the vibraphone can be made faster or slower.

The vibraphone is struck with felt or wool beaters. The player uses two beaters when he is playing melodies; and four, six or even eight beaters when playing chords. When a chord is played, the propellors take the sound and by pushing it down into the tubes beneath, keep the chord sounding a long time.

41

The *celesta* looks something like a small upright piano. The player sits at a keyboard, and fingers the instrument the same as a piano. When the player pushes the keys, hammers move and strike metal plates, instead of strings as on the piano.

Some people say the tone is like the glockenspiel, since both the celesta and glockenspiel use metal bars. However, the tone of the celesta is much more mellow and delicate. This is due partly to the wooden resonators found under each metal bar. The sound is so pleasant, sweet, and clear that it reminds the listener of the tinkle of tiny silver bells.

The celesta was invented by Auguste Mustel of Paris. The famous composer, Tchaikovsky, heard about the instrument. He had one made and sent to Russia in secret, so no one would know about it. Then he wrote a part for it in the *Dance of the Sugar Plum Fairy* from his famous *Nutcracker Suite.* Everyone was surprised and pleased with the instrument. Listen to the *Dance of the Sugar Plum Fairy.* Don't you think the celesta was a good choice to play the part of the fairy?

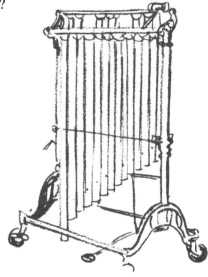

The *chimes* are another type of keyboard percussion. Like the other keyboard percussion instruments, they have definite pitch. They consist of a set of metal tubes hung like a piano keyboard from a metal frame. The longer tubes produce the lower notes and the shorter tubes the higher notes. They are struck with a wooden mallet and sound much more like real bells than the glockenspiel or celesta. Their part usually calls for a simple melody or long tones with rests in between. The tone of the chimes lasts a long time. If they are played quickly, the sound of one note is still ringing when another is struck. Listen to the *1812 Overture* by Tchaikovsky to hear chimes being played. Sometimes real bells in big churches are heard on recordings of this piece.

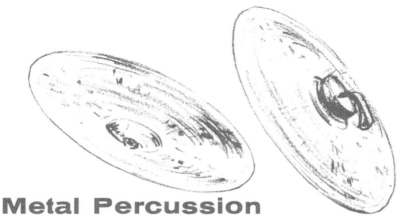

Metal Percussion

Cymbals are a pair of hollowed-out brass plates which give a big crashing effect when struck together. They came to Europe from Asia. In fact, the best cymbals that can be bought today are Turkish cymbals. The Zildjian family of Istanbul make the best cymbals. The exact formula for the cymbals has been a secret of the Zildjians for over three hundred years.

Cymbals are used for dramatic effects. This means that the composer wants to scare you, surprise you, or make sure that something in the music comes to your attention. Cymbals are also often used at the *climax,* or high point, of a section of music. The composer, however, does not use the cymbals all the time. The sound of cymbals crashing away throughout a whole piece of music would soon be dull and uninteresting.

Cymbals are played in a number of ways. They are brought together to make a big crash—the sound most of us remember when we think of cymbals. If the crash is to sound a long time, the player will hold the cymbals out in front of him, so that the air in front of him is put into motion by the vibrating cymbals. Sometimes the player will play a crash, and then he will hold the cymbals against him. If this happens, you know that the composer wanted the sound of the cymbals to stop immediately after the crash. Sometimes a

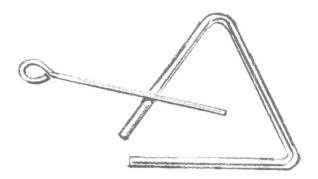

drummer will strike a single cymbal with a snare drum stick or a timpani stick. At another time, a roll will be played. One cymbal is held by a person or a cymbal holder, and the player rolls on the cymbal the same as he would on a drum. Or, cymbals can be clashed together as fast as possible to produce still another effect.

When used in pairs, cymbals are usually held by leather straps or handles. However, if you remember the picture of the trap set, you also remember that they were held on a special holder, and that two of them were played by using a foot pedal. Many times you will see a cymbal fastened to the top of a bass drum. With the right hand, the drummer beats the drum, while with the left hand, he clashes a cymbal to the one on his drum. This allows the bass drummer to play cymbals and bass drum at the same time.

The *triangle* is a small piece of steel bent into the shape of a triangle. The triangle is not completely closed, however, so that the vibrations can travel easily when it is struck. It is played with a small metal bar. The triangle has no definite pitch, but blends easily with the rest of the orchestra. Even though it is a tiny instrument, its sound is easily heard. Nothing must touch the triangle as it is played, or it will not sound. For this reason, it is usually hung from a string or some kind of holder.

The *gong* is an instrument that looks like a big round plate of hammered metal. It makes a low, brassy, and mysterious sound when struck. Sometimes its strange quality is enough to send chills up and down our spines, particularly if it is used in background music for an exciting movie or television show.

A gong is usually hung from a cord. It should be set into vibration before it is struck. This is done by priming it (starting it to vibrate) by tapping it very quietly with the beater or finger before striking it. The beater should have a heavy metal inside covered with several layers of felt to bring out the tones. Some gongs in Japanese temples are so sensitive that they are set into motion when touched with a wet thumb.

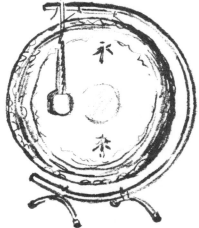

The gong started with the Greeks. Alexander the Great carried it into Asia, where it became part of the Buddhist religion. There are two types—those with a definite pitch and those with no definite pitch. In our western music we use the gong with no definite pitch.

The gong that came from China is called the *tam-tam*. No one really seems to know why. Composers call for either gong or tam-tam on the music they write. Do not make the mistake of mixing up the tam-tam with the tom-tom.

46

Other Percussion Instruments

No matter what part the composer writes, the drummers are expected to play the music. Sometimes the things they are called upon to play are quite unusual. Here is a list of a few unusual effects that can be called for:

Wood blocks	Whip
Slap stick	Sand blocks
Sleigh bells	Slide whistle
Jingle clogs	Bird whistle
Whistles	Hand and feet pounding
Auto horns	Dog bark
Ship's bell	Police whistle
Pistol shots	Horses hoofs

You may want to listen to Haydn's *Toy Symphony* to hear how one composer put the percussion players to work.

The Beat of the Drum

By now, you probably realize just how important a good percussion player is to any band or orchestra. Not only must he have a good sense of rhythm, but he must understand and appreciate the different tone colors the percussion instruments can produce. He must be able to jump from instrument to instrument within the percussion section and perform well on each.

The percussion player must have exactly the right touch. If a loud cymbal crash is called for in the music, he must supply it. If a delicate touch of the triangle is called for, he must be sure to strike gently. If a booming timpani roll is part of the music, he must roll loudly. He must be very exact, and he needs to have perfect muscle and nerve control. Percussion is the spice of music, and the spice must be added in just the right amount.

You have read about all kinds of percussion from the most primitive instruments to those used today. You have also learned that the drums are only a part of this big section of the band or orchestra. Even though the percussion instruments have been with us a very long time, today, as before, one of the most exciting sounds is *the beat of the drum!*.

48

ABOUT THE AUTHOR

Robert W. Surplus, a native of Gouldsboro, Pennsylvania, has been active in music education almost twenty years. He has had experience in every phase of music education in the public schools, and has taught all age levels from kindergarten through graduate school. Formerly Supervisor of Music at Red Lion, Pennsylvania, Associate Professor at Shippensburg State College, Shippensburg, Pennsylvania, and Instructor at Teachers College, Columbia University, he is at present an Assistant Professor in the College of Education, University of Minnesota. A graduate of Susquehanna University with a Bachelor of Science degree and of Teachers College, Columbia with a Master of Arts degree, he is presently completing the requirements for a doctorate at Columbia University.

ABOUT THE ARTIST

George Overlie is remarkably well-equipped to illustrate books for young people. An experienced artist, he has his own studio and does free-lance assignments for publishing companies, advertising agencies, and a variety of commercial clients. He is also a frequent cover contributor for the *Minneapolis Sunday Tribune Picture Magazine.* Mr. Overlie has illustrated over twenty-five books, and he finds his greatest satisfaction when working on books for young people. He studied art in New York City at the Phoenix School of Design and at the Workshop School. At present, he resides in St. Louis Park, Minnesota, with his wife and three children.

We specialize in publishing quality books for
young people. For a complete list please write

LERNER PUBLICATIONS COMPANY

241 First Avenue North, Minneapolis, Minnesota 55401